Dark Pool

Ben Howard

Ben Howard

salmonpoetry

Other Books by Ben Howard

POETRY

Father of Waters: Poems 1965-1976
(Abattoir Editions: University of Nebraska at Omaha, 1979)

Northern Interior: Poems 1975-1982
(The Cummington Press, 1986)

Lenten Anniversaries: Poems 1982-1989
(The Cummington Press, 1990)

Midcentury
(Salmon Publishing, 1997)

PROSE

The Pressed Melodeon: Essays on Modern Irish Writing
(Story Line Press, 1996)

Published in 2004 by
Salmon Publishing Ltd.,
Cliffs of Moher, County Clare, Ireland
Website: www.salmonpoetry.com
email: info@salmonpoetry.com

ISBN 1 903392 32 2

Cover artwork: Detail from "Dome" by Robert Turner. Photo by Brian Oglesbee
Cover design & typesetting: Siobhán Hutson

for Robin

Acknowledgments

Acknowledgments are due to the following publications in which some of these poems were previously published:

The Amicus Journal, Chelsea, The Cortland Review, Dharma Connection, The Formalist, Poetry, Poetry Ireland Review, Prairie Schooner, The Recorder, Sewanee Review, Shenandoah, Southern Humanities Review, and *TriQuarterly.*

"Lines for the Makers" appeared as a limited edition, printed by Jerry Reddan and published by the Tangram Press (Berkeley, 1998).

"Lincoln's Hands" appeared in *Voices in the Gallery: Writers on Art*, ed. Grant Holcomb (University of Rochester Press, 2001).

Contents

III

IV

Sentence

i.m. Marion Howard (1905-1971)

Where are you now, if not within this hand
That moves as steadily across the page
As you in life processed within the span
Allotted you, your sentence and your song?

I

Dark Pool

Tomorrow something new may cross my path
But today I write to you from Dublin City,
Whose name, as you well know, is anything
But new. Along with torcs and other relics,
The Danes who lived and moved in these environs
Left behind an image and a name.
Whatever I may think when I look out
On Georgian squares beset by noisy traffic,
The Danish eyes that fastened on this landscape
Perceived in it a place of murky water,
To which they gave the Danish name for *dark*
And the Danish name for *pool*, which in the dark,
Unending stream of naming and re-naming
Became *dubh linn*, its Irish counterpart.
And so I write to you this Monday morning
From the Dark Pool, whose air is often damp,
As though its early name had lingered on,
Exuding into air no longer Danish
Or altogether Irish something wet
And dark—the residue of habitation
But also of the languages that came
And went, the words no weightier than ours
That now are part of that unseen deposit
Which lies on walls and lanes and kitchen gardens
And sometimes smothers what it claims to know.

II

    Henry Street. Not recently or ever
Have I known any personage whose name
Became a street or avenue or lane,
Much less a thoroughfare or monument.
Some names are monstrous, others visible
Only under lens or microscope.
Whoever Henry was, his name attests
More to someone's estimate of value
Than to a lasting memory of Henry,
Who is not technically anonymous
But is, if I may venture such a judgment,
Functionally extinct. As for his name,
It has, I think, the status of a leaf,
Albeit one in tin, securely fastened
And seeming on a late-September day
As likely to survive him as those statues
Bearing the names *Parnell, Moore, O'Connell.*
Yet only yesterday, when I picked up
A history of the Easter insurrection,
I read that at the peak of their rebellion,
The joists and plaster of the G.P.O.
Crumbling on their dream of Irish freedom,
The poet-rebels tunnelled from that building
And into Henry Street, there to establish
A last defense against ordained defeat,
A stay against inevitable surrender.
What do I know, I asked myself not once
But twice, so sweeping was my ignorance,
So deaf my ears to overtones of meaning,
Which in the Irish psyche resonate
As clearly as the Angelus at twilight,
Despite the bleats of cell-phones on the sidewalks,
The near-incessant roar of Dublin traffic.

III

Where are you now, that I should write to you
From this bewildered city? I call it that
To capture if I can its quick-step tempo,
Its harsh brasses and, no less than that,
Its rattling drums. I mean no disrespect
To the Dark Pool nor to its thousand years
Of history, its celebrated streets
Where authors in their cups and noisy poets
Maintained the gardens of their verbal Eden;
Where untold creatures clamoured to be named
And giants suited to that grand vocation
Threw out a dozen sumptuous appellations
For every beast that lumbered into view.
Dark Pool indeed! City of the Names,
I might have called it—names for enemies
And friends, cousins and acquaintances,
Passions and their objects, furtive feelings,
And all the dreck not spoken of in public
But named within the confines of the heart
And later brought to light. Bewilderment
Is not too strong a word for that emotion
Which sometimes overtakes me on these sidewalks,
Congested as they are with men and women
In earnest attitudes and in a hurry.
Such was the case one Friday afternoon
When everyone was headed to a bar
Or seemed to be, and I was out of step,
A foreigner with letters on his mind,
The ones I should have written earlier
To friends and family, retailing stories
Heard in the pubs or overheard in buses
Or clipped from pages of the *Irish Times*.
Those anecdotes more present in my mind

Than what was happening before my eyes,
I found myself accompanying the crowd
Into a pub whose name I can't remember,
Though I can see its stools and leather benches,
Its swirling smoke, its animated faces.
Maybe it was the Dublin intonation,
The *tink*'s and *grand*'s and *brilliant*'s in the air,
The talk that was the sound track to the dramas
Occurring in the booths or at the tables—
Whatever it may have been, that dense profusion
Was like a storm, a bout of ugly weather
That I had wandered into, unprepared
And not well suited to negotiate.
Pausing at the counter, undecided
Whether to add more wind to that commotion
Or leave the way I came, as yet unnoticed,
I felt a word expanding in my mind
And pressing for release. The word was *publish*,
Untainted by its modern acceptation
And meaning, as of old, to interject
A private truth into the public body,
To make one's feelings known in public forum.
And as I entertained that potent word,
So rich in consequence and implication,
I found my tensions easing and my mind
Reflecting on the fabric I had entered,
Which someone aptly named a *public house*,
A shelter, if you like, for *publishers*,
However circumspect their revelations
Or cautious their impromptu publications.
Lifting my pint of Guinness, newly pulled
And primly handsome in its priestly collar,
I took my place among the publishers
And offered to the stranger on my right,
A nodding lad, inclined to conversation,
The essence of my thoughts on Irish weather.

IV

What is a name if not a bolt of fabric,
Its shape and aspect tailored and adorned
To suit the common good? One Friday morning
I lifted up mine eyes to the horizon
Whence came no help and only a little light,
The weather being damp and overcast,
The sky a dull and unrelenting grey.
Against that muted glow, revolving slowly,
A yellow crane attended to its business,
Some heavy object dangling from its cables.
What caught my eye and held my rapt attention
Was propped above the weights behind the cab,
Its presence no less bright for being small.
It was, I saw, the flag of the Republic,
Its triple colours flapping in the wind.
Imagining the man who climbed the ladder
And crawled out on the beam to mount it there
I felt a shuddering of vertigo,
As though it were myself who set that emblem
Of nationhood and long-sought independence
Aloft above a busy, fabled city
Which may or may not notice or regard it
Or find in orange, green, and neutral white
Its true identity. I looked away
And down, no native and no patriot
But stirred to wonder by a piece of cloth,
Whose form was changing even as I watched,
Its meaning not to be interpreted
But left to cast its net on crowded streets
And engines racing to the latest fire.

V

When does a common thing become a name
To be pronounced, intoned, interpreted,
Until the presence of the thing itself
Dissolves within the noise the noun is making?
That question crossed my mind as I was walking
In Stephen's Green on a Sunday afternoon,
Remembering the time I heard the word
Collective, liking its liquid consonants,
Its quiet vowels and its gentle burst
Of energy, as though a cloud had spoken.
Little did I know that in a word
So pleasing to the ear and to the tongue
There lived a history of violence,
A chronicle of griefs and deprivations,
Of manacles and chains and executions,
All in the name of some *collective* good
Which justified the evils it propounded.
What faith remains when names replace the things
Entrusted to their care? That afternoon,
The ducks in Stephen's Green were diving. Dipping
Into the water and out, in quest of tidbits,
They fit, or so I thought, their names: they *ducked*
And *ducked* again, their comic act restoring
An old congruity of word and thing,
As though the first to name those feathered shapes
Had got it right: had said what he had seen.

VI

Who shall be nameless, goes the politic
Expression, leaving us to conjure out
Of reference and tone the missing persons,
Who may be nameless to their dying days
But nonetheless appear as living shades
Acting and reacting on that stage
We set before our eyes. What matter, now,
If swarthy Jack was really Anthony
And winsome Jill was really Madeline?
I think of them this morning, Jack and Jill,
Who sat across from me, as nearly joined
As any could be on a public bus
Jouncing down a street in Sandymount.
Oblivious of me, as of those others
Who read their paperbacks or sat in silence,
Jack and Jill were visibly enthralled
By what they had created, hand in hand
And lip on lip, its presence palpable.
I tried myself to be oblivious
But found my gaze returning to their faces,
So rapt were they in worship of their god.
That was twenty years ago or more.
And though those devotees have long since tumbled
Into a vale I'd rather not envision,
They stay in memory as in a vase,
Where dried stems may yet arrest attention
And dried blooms remain without a name.

VII

They're waiting for a day or two, my friends
In Templeogue, to name their newborn daughter.
Will she be Lily? Deirdre? Margaretta?
They're saying nothing, letting us remain
Pleasantly in suspense, and letting her
Who presently is nameless have her day,
Unburdened by the garment she will wear
On every future day, the heavy ulster
Which may or may not suit her temperament,
Her way of speaking or her coloration,
But will, for life, be hers to don or carry.
So let me celebrate, this Sunday morning,
The blessed freedom of an unnamed child.
And let me recognise, as best I can,
That infant's counterpart, who may yet dwell
In every mortal frame that walks the planet
And every smattering of skin and bone
That lies beneath a name inscribed in granite.
To write a letter to that nameless one
Who in myself appears from time to time,
Unmarked by passion or adversity
And all the ills to which the flesh is prone—
To write a letter, asking her forgiveness
Or failing that, her tolerance and grace,
Could be the occupation of a lifetime,
A project suited to my later years,
A correspondence worthy of the effort.
For now, I lift my cup to that small soul,
So full of cries but empty of a name,
Who soon enough will have not one but three,
Each name a gate, a portico, a window.

VIII

How loftily the pundits speculate
About a future no one will decipher
Even in retrospect, employing names
To do the work of knowing and unknowing,
The shaping and reshaping of the story.
What Jane will call a *splendid revolution*
Will seem to Joan a *spurious rebellion*
And facts themselves will gradually unravel
As sweaters do, their yarns at last returning
Into that primal state from whence they came.
Yet if I may join that happy band
Of prophets, panelists, and charlatans
Who claim to have a purchase on the future,
Allow me to envision Dublin City
In fifty years, its National Museum
Still the same, though newly stocked with cell phones
And other relics of our present time.
Its air will be more redolent of Progress,
Its Liffey even filthier than now,
Its urban essence all too effable.
As for the culture that sustained itself
On words and stout, as others have on wine,
What will become of it? My guess, as good
As anyone's, is that its bronze memorials,
Its Kavanagh and Anna Livia,
Its lanky Jimmy with his walking stick,
Will outlast all of us, a fitting tribute
To writers whom the world has deigned to honour.
But as for what those Publishers have published,
Those writers written in their finer hours,
I see it too as gradually disbanding,
As though the names that gathered on a page
Or in a room had gone their separate ways

And every text were headed for perdition.
Looking down this evening at the Liffey,
I see the waves dispersing on the quay,
The wakes dissolving in the fleeting light,
And wonder if those poems learnt by heart
Or cherished under glass in dustless rooms
Are any more coherent or substantial.
If not, then let the *dubh linn* claim its own,
The Names give up their portions to the stream.
And let it flow as mightily as water,
This language that is neither yours nor mine
But enters and inhabits us, its colours
As varied as the colours of the world,
Its lanes and crescents, channels and canals
As trafficked or as desolate as those
The eye encounters on its daily rounds
And shores against incipient erasure.

Leavings

Today I write from Meg's Uptown Café
On Castle Street, where someone's scarred guitar
Keeps company with someone's violin,
The two of them suspended from their pegs
On plaster that could use a coat of paint.
Who built those instruments and who performed
Sonatas and partitas, gigues and fugues,
Or, more likely, reels and Kerry slides,
Are matters for a morning's contemplation.
Even as I sip my bitter tea
And make the best of under-scrambled eggs,
I'm thinking of an air by Paganini,
In which the pure, impassioned violin
Ascends above the chords of the guitar
And occupies an atmosphere of longing
But in the end, as if to gratify
The need of all things light to live on earth,
Comes down in one reverberant cadenza.
It's raining now, as often in Tralee.
And as those anxious walkers on the pavement
Bow their heads to meet the brutal weather,
I'm hearing yet again that high cadenza
As though it were a trace in these environs,
A relic no more visible than want
Or memory, desire or speculation,
But nonetheless as present as the stench
Of cigarettes, those odours from the kitchen,
These bits of bacon cooling on my plate.

Children of Lir

At Siamsa Tíre, they're featuring the tale
Of children taken by an evil spell
Out of their downy beds and human forms
And cast as plaintive swans upon the waters,
There to remain until a saintly bell
Reclaim them from the lakes, no longer young
But still intact in every noble limb
And speaking softly in a human tongue.
The lights go down. The orchestra unfolds
A melody evocative of loss
But also of recovery and joy.
And when the actors, after many turns
Across the stage, declaim their sculpted lines,
The language that they speak with such conviction
Is not the English of my childhood
Nor of the pubs in neighbourly Tralee
But something more indigenous than that—
A mother tongue, whose fricatives and vowels
Conjure out of air a vanished culture
And banish for a time the English god
Whose heart is beating everywhere but here.
They could be swans themselves, those Irish phrases
Rising from a simulated landscape
And telling as of old a likely story,
A parable of suffering and silence
Which has no denouement nor happy ending
Except it be this moment, where the past
Appears in costume, singing an ancient song
And dancing to a tune not yet forgotten.

Holy Water

Was it a drink I wanted? Walking past
The public benches and the public toilets,
The roses in the garden, worse for wear
But still exuberant on trellises,
I turned into a churchyard, where the stones
Took on the slanted light of early evening
And voices softened, not in reverence
So much as confidence or privacy.
Strolling through the shade of the cathedral,
I found myself positioned by a wall
From which a faucet jutted, featureless
But for the metal sign above the spout.
Holy Water. Not a caption, really,
Nor yet a cataloguer's designation
But something more insidious than that,
A sort of invitation to a party
Or more respectfully, a gathering
To which I had no conscious inclination.
Speaking in Roman characters, it held me
Long enough to wonder where it came from,
That latent spirit cloistered in a pipe,
Its fluent cadence silenced by a valve
Though primed to be released at any moment.
All it would have taken was a turn,
A counter-clockwise motion of the hand.
What was it stopped me? Say it was a sense
Of something tangible behind my shoulder,
By which I mean no priest or risen ghost,
Much less a stern protector of the State,
But something I'd brought with me to Tralee,
A figment of a once and future longing.
Would that it might sustain me or be gone.
Would that I might pass and leave no trace.

Fidelities

What heart can know itself?
—Anthony Hecht

I

Coal dust thickens on my palate. Eight
o'clock: too early for the gardeners
and the workman with his scythe, who yesterday
cut wide swathes through weeds and knee-high grass.
Too early, too, for that conglomerate
of lies and vows, of true and false desires,
to fashion its imaginings from clay,
or wreak its mess, or work its synthesis.
Call it the heart. Or call it nothing more
than compost piled at the garden's edge,
contaminated silage. Now to look
inward is to watch an untilled field
lighten and darken like an overture
whose instruments have more than they can manage.
The score is treacherous. And each mistake
leaves that much more to ferret and unfold
from such small findings as avail themselves,
their secrets hidden in a turn of phrase
or trick of harmony, their fragile poise
lost and recovered as their form evolves.

II

This Irish dampness strews its melancholy
sweetness over the fields. Those cattle nosing
up to the fence, swishing the flies away,
could teach me, once and for all, how unavailing
and how ungracious appetite can be,
lumbering toward its apple-branch and choosing
nothing but what's before it. And every stray
desire, every random hankering
held back or satisfied, as it may happen.
Where will it end, that lust for foreign things—
or things made foreign by a change of light,
a shift of wind? Returning to the tonic,
the cadences confirm their origin,
call out their names. The coloratura sings
on key. And here, as if to clear its throat,
the northern sky grows brilliant, seraphic—
before relapsing to a common gray,
which in its steady dampness may appease
an appetite for permanence and vows
and in its bleakness pass for constancy.

III

Beneath these fluctuating waves, those currents
persist in changing light. The reeds hold still;
the evening contracts. To look beneath
this surface is to wait upon a friend
who will in time appear, his coat and pants
dripping, his eyes intelligent and tranquil.
What he will tell you of a changing earth
whose changes have no purpose and no end
will not suffice. Nor will his recitations,
thrown out above the water's ostinato,
do more than guide you to that other scene,
that nightly theatre of unformed thought,
where characters in livid conversations
remake their lives; where lovers come and go
in semblances and parodies of action,
and brutal acts advance a shapeless plot.
Call it your heart. Or call it your asylum,
its hours measured by a muffled gong,
its speech the bleatings of a foreign tongue
spoken in haste, under a foreign emblem.

Remembering Galway

That city where the streets are sinuous
and wind, as if predestined, to the river:
why does it come back to me this morning,
as though its smoky pubs and crowded shops

were daubs of paint, and I were but a canvas
receptive to the gestures of desire?
Even now, the sight of swans returning,
their stable forms afloat amidst the cups

and sticks, their necks recumbent on their breasts,
could be the mere projection of a mind
replete with specious emblems of repose
and freighted with its own uncertain notions.

Yet even now the memory of gusts
on Claddagh Quay, the reek of salty wind,
and the one red house—distinct among the greys
and bobbing in the water's undulations—

take on their own solidities and causes.
That was an artist's house, my friend explains.
The artist moved away; but what remains
is hard as glaze, as real as painted vases.

For the Record

Ripeness is all, but here in mid-October
in New York State, a vivid decadence
is all or nearly all, the hillsides red
with sumac, beech, and maple. *Come and see*,

the Buddha said; and having seen, remember
the purple sedum in its late florescence,
the cardinal flower long since gone to seed
but upright still, as though a memory

of brilliance could sustain it through the winter.
Remember, too, the afternoon in Dublin,
the German couple crossing Stephen's Green,
no longer young but walking arm in arm

past the men and women in their twenties
who lay entwined or basked beside the fountain.
And see yourself, a watcher in the sunshine
of late July, a devotee of form

who saw the cloud-shapes changing by the minute
above the trees, and honed his chosen phrases,
as though each shape were frozen in his clauses
and each indited word were cut in granite.

Elegy

For Fred Hanna's Bookshop,
now Eason-Hanna's

The name remains but nothing of the floor-
to-ceiling shelves, the dusty intimacy.
Now the aisles are wide, the rubrics neat.
The checkout clerk waits by her computer.

Call it Progress. Call it What is Good
for Commerce. Not so good for you and me,
who came here to be neighboured by a culture
whose face was plain, whose heart was writ on paper.

Not that every author pleased our palates
nor that their world was kind, benevolent,
or just. Rather that it spoke to us,
its voice now hoarse, now sweet, but always human.

II

The Intellect of Man

Always to be setting down in words
such sights as cardinals and neighbours' cats—

those partners in a scheme for which no name
will quite suffice—or capturing in phrases

made for the occasion some occurrence
that happened in the yard or in the mind

or somewhere in between: is it a habit,
no better than a gait or tic or gesture,

or is it more than that: a noble art
for which no sacrifice or contribution

will ever be too great? Consider Yeats,
who thought that poetry and daily life

contended for the centre of attention
in every poet's heart. Or read the lines

of Baudelaire or Shelley or Millay
and ask if poetry and equanimity

are often to be found in one sound mind
or are, like cats and cardinals, the players

in some unformed and unrelenting drama
which one day ends, though written words continue.

The Growing Poem

We cut it back, the lavish forsythia
whose branches had grown thick and interlocked,
their high arcs intertwined with untrained limbs,
blocking light and hampering the view.
How dwarfed it looks, its green insignia
returning week by week, its trunk-wood hacked
to knee-high stubs, from which resurgent stems
extend themselves, bearing a leaf or two.
I think of it this morning, reading lines
and cadences that will in time be chopped
to half their length or cut out altogether,
the opened space an aperture for light
and for such meanings as reside in zones
not clogged with word or matter. Managed, cropped,
and vulnerable to every sort of weather,
the growing poem seeks its perfect height,
as though its syllables were born of soil
and circumstance, its predicates of water,
its eloquence of rain and wintry air
replete with light and redolent of toil.

Perennials

Cut back, the gardens once again recede
to what they were before the wild buddleia
impaired our view, presenting to the eye
its own exuberant stems, its lilac mansions.
Cut down, the once-imperial cardinal flower
no longer calls attention to itself
nor do those gray, aggressive artemisia
occupy a ground that might have been
their own, so lasting was their residence,
so prevalent their spreading silver mounds.
Would that you and I, grown slightly older,
might find our counterparts in quinces pruned
and roots protected by decaying leaves.
Would that we might certify ourselves
as occupants of once and future gardens,
our worst proclivities deposited
beneath a hacked but still-resilient plant,
our memories encased in husks and cauls
or lifted like those dahlias, two by two,
and stored in sacks, as if there were no winter.

Currencies

The sky will write no signatures this morning
and post no bills. Something communicates
its loss in days as overcast as this,
the air so thick and damp as to diminish
commerce between free thought and these returning
leaves, this light that asks for nothing. Rates
change; the sidewalks crack; the happiness
recounted once too often turns to cash,
its graven face negotiable but torn
and mutilated by the dailiness
that falls between the moment and its ghost,
the night experienced and the night recalled.
Better to store the moment in its urn,
the cherished touch in silent consciousness,
the day in speechless praise. Or count the cost
in memories depleted or annulled
by alphabet and stanza. Here and now,
the lilacs have gone by; the purple phlox
reach from the ditch; and in its cloister *vox
humana* deigns to record or disavow.

The Swinging Door

I. Reticence

What is it but an envelope devised
to shelter those invisible desires,
those petty bigotries and rancid fears,
which would, if not protected, be exposed

for what they are? What is it but a bolt,
which keeps the stores of memory secure,
lest your house be looted by that burglar
who knows your slightest move, your subtlest habit,

your grossest fault? But what your barriers
have held at bay is not that predator
alone, nor yet the tireless voyeurs,

but that constrained intruder in your heart,
whose business is to see you as you are,
however much you keep yourself apart.

II. *Release*

What have you wanted more than that release
from isolation? Even a fleeting touch
on fingertip or wrist extends the reach
of your awareness to a foreign place

beyond this cell of silent contemplation,
so spacious in its way but so immune
to news of others' triumphs and misfortune.
Why then do you recoil in agitation

from inquiries and friendly overtures,
as though they might contaminate the pure
and noiseless air, the dustless atmospheres

in which, if you could have them, you would live,
your element a rectifying fire,
your silence no less potent than your love?

III. Shutters

In you, as in the closing of a chest
replete with cardigans and blocks of cedar
and lending to its ambience an odour
at once arcane and quietly robust,

I see the gestures of a temperament
responsive to itself as to the season,
as eager to be shut as to contain,
all summer long, each neatly folded garment.

Where will it end, that cycle of disclosure
and closing-up, advancement and retreat?
Within the moments of your timed exposure

I see a lens preparing to be shuttered,
as though the truest movement of your heart
were systole, your truest words unuttered.

IV. Interrogations

Is it for me that you have worn a mask,
its fixed mouth and inward-turning eye
suggesting caution or humility
or something in between? And when I ask

questions of the face that I encounter,
day by day and year by passing year,
is it a looking-glass or two-way mirror
that you present to me, its hidden centre

there, or never there? Were you to answer,
I would consider what you had to say,
as though it held the truth of your desire,

wondering all the while if what I'd heard
were your confession or your kind reply,
your artful parry or your final word.

Lessons

for my father

Late August finds tomatoes on the vine
      and in the juniper the fine
net of a caterpillar. Say
      which of the signs of fall
will turn up first. Well enough
      to see the treeline, green
as if in Eden. Here, as if
      I needed it, the light
takes on an orange tint
      and a slant that summons memories
of fallen leaves. And you, wherever you
      may be, assume your rightful place
at the centre of my thought: old teacher,
      tell me again why days and nights
shorten and why your own
      ended when they did. And tell me
what it is that makes the bark
      of a neighbour's dog sound clear and cold,
as though it stood apart from dying things
      and its shape were cut in stone.

Forecast

for Alexander

One day soon *Lobelia cardinalis*,
now a purple badge against the dried
cypress chips, a spreading fleur-de-lis,
will rise into the tallest of those plants
we chose last year, the brilliant cardinal flower.
And one day soon, whatever we began
the autumn afternoon when you were born
will reach a height I haven't yet imagined,
as you proceed to your majority
and that prodigious plant which sons and fathers
grow in clay or loam assumes a shape
and coloration yet to be conceived
by you or me. Call it maturity,
that shedding of the last protective foliage
and that unveiling. Call it what you will,
it's happening to us as well as you,
even as the workers in the garden
unload new soil and loose into the air
a high, unearthly, celebratory shower.

July, 1997

Lincoln's Hands

Life Mask and Hands of Abraham Lincoln
Leonard Wells Volk (American, 1828-1895)

Cast in bronze and silent under glass,
      they keep their peace amidst
the landscapes, the chat of passers-by.
      The left lies flat, as on
a letter; the fingers of the right
      curl around a handle.
How delicate but how decisive
      these sculpted fingers look,
as if they held, in lasting balance,
      the mollifying touch
and, when warranted, the will to strike
      or sever. *I now wish*
to make the personal acknowledgement
      that you were right and I
was wrong. So he wrote to General
      Grant on July 13,
1863. As though they flowed
      within these metal veins,
his accurate phrases cross my mind,
      their courtly eloquence
and candour undiminished. Tell me
      if this is how we last,
our words no more erasable than bronze
      or faces carved in stone.

A Given Name

for Joanne and Gary Mensinger

i

Maquoketa. I think I heard it first
out of my father's mouth. A quiet town
in Iowa, it left me unimpressed
but for its name, which like a pleasing tune
heard on the radio, installed itself,
its savour growing stronger through the years.
Speaking *Maquoketa* now, I find myself
removed to where I lopped on wooden stairs
and fed fresh raisins to a cocker spaniel,
my mother vacuuming, my sister building
dolls from hollyhocks. Each syllable
could be a raisin, too, and each unfolding
consonant a sweetness on the tongue,
the name itself an elegiac song.

ii

Des Moines. Clinton. Davenport. Dubuque.
As easily as breathing, I intone
those lasting names, as though no loss or heartbreak
had ever happened. Closed and long since gone,
Van Allen's grand department store in Clinton
has left its Louis Sullivan facade,
a convoluted signature in stone.
Part-Celtic, part-Corinthian, its dated
elegance recalls a finer time,
when cities spoke from throbbing civic hearts.
Today the shoppers, stocking home and farm,
avail themselves of bargains at the K-Marts,
forsaking Penney's and Montgomery Ward's.
What stays are names and opulent facades.

iii

I hear them in the morning and the evening,
as though they signified familiar rooms
in musty public buildings: *Bath*, *Corning*,
Binghamton, *Elmira*. Foreign names
at first, they've lost their colours. Twenty years
of hearing them have made their flavours dull,
their structures no more striking than the spires
of friendly churches, charitable and local.
But will there come a time when I endow
those common places with the same affection
as now I sometimes feel when *Iowa*
comes up in revery or conversation
or makes its way, as patiently as bees,
into the papers or the evening news?

iv

I can't call back the years nor legislate,
by any act of naming, my return
to that remembered, half-imagined state
when name and home and family were one.
Nor can I make of *Iowa* a shelter
impervious to fashion or assault,
nor build of empty properties an altar,
nor carve from words a temporal retreat.
And yet I do just that, in speech and thought,
as though the names *Maquoketa* and *Clinton*,
uttered in reverence, could muster out
the tutelary spirit of a town
and by the glory of a given name
bestow the passing credence of a dream.

Early Music

Here in the chill of winter,
My furnace thrusting heat
Into my drafty study,
I hear the muted beat
Of a Scottish melody,
The muted, pulsing beat.

Unknown to me, those players
Plucking lute and cittern,
That passionate soprano
Plying a Scottish tune
Over an ostinato,
A plaintive Scottish tune.

Unknown to me, my own
Hunger for a warm
And fluent melody
Coursing within its form,
Blood renewing body,
Form remaking form.

Greta

All day she lies
beneath the pin oak, leashed
to a post, her space defined,
her world encompassed by a nylon cord.

Looking away from us, she sees
those spruce trees in their mid-September colours,
the lilies still in bloom,
and, from time to time,
the neighbour's yellow cat, who keeps

his distance, stepping lightly.
What passes through her mind,
we wonder, watching her sphinx-like calm,
her easy vigilance.

And what, if anything, can we,
her keepers, know of that awareness,
which senses each incursion
and sniffs each unfamiliar,
uninvited odour?

And when she greets us, tail
swishing, tongue expectant,
does she not see a portion of ourselves
which we ourselves will never see,

though we outlive her lapping tongue,
her black, recumbent body?

A Winter Fire

i

Just yesterday, as if to inform myself
with news I'd made an effort to forget,
I listened to some chewings in my roof,
some feet across the rafters. What I'd thought
immutable—or built to last the decade—
was showing its unstable character
and scattering its dust above my head.
It might have been a lawsuit or a fire
or merely a new inflection in a voice
protesting permanence. Into the day's
apparent peace it sent its hungry mice
to eat my joists and short my circuitries.
Under the ribs of my apparent calm
it stirred the torments of another time

ii

What matters in these early morning hours
is not those fears and animosities,
those rankling slights and unrelenting worries
which block my light and taint my diaries
but what arrives half-noticed, half-expected:
a chill in the air, a sudden darkening
across the sill, a wrinkle in my forehead.
Were I to read those signs as souls returning
from some remote dominion of the dead
or find in them an emblem for those hurts
which are, for good or ill, our daily bread,
I'd miss the point entirely. Out of the night's
emptiness come inklings of a morning
devoid of thought and innocent of meaning.

iii

Insolent, unseemly, avaricious,
those intimations of a new disorder
in mind or body, flesh or consciousness,
intrude upon the pleasures of the hour
and the languor of a Sunday afternoon.
Talking unguardedly and sipping wine
on a friend's deck, I felt a sudden pain
beneath my belt, as though a tree had fallen
over a power line. Then less and less,
and the throbbing stopped. The conversation spread
its coat of meanings over that awareness
of something gone awry. Whatever dread
it wakened in my bowels and my brain
dissolved in words, its origin unknown.

iv

Merely to call them by their rightful names
is to see them as they are: *anxiety*,
unrest, *unease*. No longer will the pseudonyms
suffice. Contentment is not serenity,
nor anger rage, nor perturbation torment.
Awake at four, I heard the rise and fall
of my own breath and felt a hot resentment,
a tightened jaw, a pulsing in my temple.
What were the names for those indignities
which burned below the grate of conscious thought?
I called them *insults*, *lies*, and *travesties*
and drifted back to sleep. But what I brought
out of the heat of that nocturnal fire
came back to warm me in a winter hour.

Winter Night

The full moon emerges
through thinning cirrus clouds.
Over the spruce's top
it hangs, remote, unharmed.

My feet and hands are cold.
On the packed snow my soles
make squeaks but leave no tracks.
I know I am alive.

III

Come and See

Accompanied by hosta and impatiens,
Shakyamuni sits beneath the tree,
Famously serene and not at all
Concerned with what a doctrineless observer
Is thinking as he looks out on his lawn,

Making of spruce and pine and wild lupine
A composition he might call his own,
Were not its parts available to all,
Its order neither human nor inhuman
Nor wholly arbitrary. *Come and see,*

The Buddha is reported to have said,
Encouraging the blasting of conceptions,
A waking to the blackbird on the lawn
Who just now flew, too quick for any mind
To organise or order into stone.

Prose Should Be Transparent

Prose should be transparent, Orwell said,
A windowpane through which that cardinal
Rooting in the leaves for fallen seeds

Can be himself and not an English phrase
Exchanged for yet another over coffee
Or formed of ink, each character a flag

Run up a pole or draped below a window
To honour that incomparable bird
Who even now has flown, unharmed, unhindered.

Remembering Peace

for Thich Nhat Hanh

Not for your renown
will I remember you

nor even for the gentle
tenor of your voice.

Over the gathered *sangha*
your voice reminded us

that *to love is to listen.*
But should the suffering

you spoke of lacerate
the ones to whom I listen,

will I remember you
at peace beside the lake,

your brown robe spread about you,
sitting as you've sat

for half a century?
And will I recall the children

you'd gathered to your side—
the strangely silent children

who sketched their alphabets
and symbols in the sand?

Rhinebeck, New York, 1995

A Discipline

Hardest of all, this month of February,
This isthmus with its snow and icy roads,
Its dripping eaves and dirty melting mounds.
How difficult to live in such a venue,
Which seems, on darker mornings, like a threshold
Before a door that will or will not open.

How urgent, then, to learn the discipline
Of living here in ugly February,
Not wanting days to end or calendars
To turn, but saying, *There you are*, *my friend*,
And *Here I am* to frozen creeks and rivers,
Which any day may melt and throw up floods.

Habits

How arrogantly they carry us
    into the pharmacy, the market,
        the bank, even the darkened bedroom,

as though we were the wafers on
    their tray, the pot of steaming tea,
        the empty cups. And we accede

most days, so innocent are we
    of their insidious intent,
        their will to make us inmates of

ourselves, incarcerate our longings,
    reduce our acts to replicas,
        our words to parodies, our smiles

to imitations. What happiness
    to send those sponsors on their way:
        to taste, at last, the tangerine,

the bowl of cereal set before us,
    the berries' ripe intelligence,
        the cup of coffee not yet cold.

Necessities

Merely to watch those juncos at the feeder,
Their language not the consonants and vowels
Of human speech but potent all the same,
Each flutter of the wings a dare or warning,

Suffices to recall him to the moment,
That watcher at the window who divides
The Better from the Best, the Not So Good
From what his shifting mind elects to value,

Forgetting that in this the present moment
Those gray-and-white arrivals at the feeder
Are taking what they need and nothing extra,
Each dip and turn a necessary gesture.

Claims

How steadily they gratify a longing
for peace of mind, despite their flickering

in each new draft, their bright inconstancy.
And now they pop and spit, as if the thought

of their dissolving had unsettled them
or left them wanting. Tapers in a tarnished,

wax-daubed candelabrum, they commend
themselves to our attention, sending up

no smoke or gas but nonetheless declaiming
in tones suggestive of another time.

Like incense they will gradually commit
their forms to formlessness, their graceful shapes

to nothing more material than the air
that even now is claiming wax and wick

and will in time appropriate that scent
which now and then resembles ripened fruit

and seems no less substantial than the drips
that now accumulate in lumps and mounds

beneath a flame that sinks as if resigning
or falling to the depths from which it came.

Lines for the Makers

The Wasp

Awake at four, I hear
the stir of traffic on the Northway,

the first birds. Intelligence
comes slowly, if at all.

Where is my father? Not
in the blue jay squawking at

this early hour. Not in the wasp,
whose curled and writhing

body, cupped and dropped
from three floors up, flies free.

The Net

Indra's net, the Buddhist calls it,
this whole of which the fly

on the lampshade and the thought
of poems, lampshades, flies

are parts. How often have I begun
again and yet again

this threading of the world's
discrete particulars, as though

inventing what in truth
was there, and always there?

Pollen

On my desk, the dictionary,
and in the air the pollen

falling from conifers on us,
the wheezing moralists,

the sneezing makers. What
is ours? What is theirs,

those Norway maples,
unconscious of their names,

which fall like pollen from
our lips, and leave

their dust on lamp and table
and every living thing?

The Library

How best to honour those
who've gone before? Establish

a statue in a corner,
a park bench near the water,

a yearly lecture? Here
their books remain, are read

now and again, or never.
Taller every year,

the pines let in the light
or hoard it. Here

the cards in the catalogue
repose, though crimped and faded.

"Continue"

What better word for what
we do?

Dare we admit, while walking
past the rooms where writers

work, have worked, are working,
that in the end, for all

their dour rigours and their dark,
methodical denials,

.the Protestants got it right: the work
and yet again the work

will root the separate self
out of its cell of thought

and make a radiant net
of pollen, wasp, and maple.

Yaddo, 1997

Westward

Why do poets in their advancing years,
When love of the word survives, but only barely,
Cleave to the long and fluid, half-prosaic line
As though it were a cable for rappelling
And not a tightrope any longer? Why do they write
As though the informing spirit had no checks
Or exigencies, no chastening vessel?
This afternoon in Prescott, Arizona,
Liz is making her travel plans, and I
Relax in the pickup, reading Carruth's long lines
That have the fluency of one who no longer cares
For the world's praise and the self's advancement,
Moving as freely as those cirrus clouds
In the Arizona sky. In truth,
I am neither old nor given to self-defeat,
But the freedom of those who no longer write for praise
Appeals to me, and the easy flow
Of Hayden's lines is a likeable illusion.
I think when I am old, when lines
Come slowly or not at all,
I will recall this piece of make-believe,
These lines so much at liberty with themselves,
This clear, unhindered western sky.

Heartwood

Is it not a second innocence,
this state of being fifty-nine,
just shy of that formidable
age of stature and attainment
if also of forgetting? Let

the chips fall, the shavings make
their mess beneath that steady blade
whose cut is deepening, whose teeth
approach a still, resistant core,
a place of origins and endings.

IV

The Holy Alls

The Burren, 1950

I

How did it happen that an Iowan
Without credentials or portfolio
Re-domiciled himself in County Clare
And having left his native ground behind him
Became its ill-prepared ambassador?
I've asked myself that question more than once,
Being myself that odd American
Or as I'm sometimes called in these environs,
The Yank who lives alone in Ballyvaughan
And sometimes can be found at Connor's pub
Sipping his whiskies with the best of them—
Or, more often, walking in the Burren,
Looking the part of someone's long-lost son.
How I might, on any given morning,
Construe the waking body I inhabit
Or greet the gander in my shaving-mirror
Or name his features, is another matter.
Stopping at the victualler's to chat
Or pausing in the market to inquire
After the health of someone's relative,
I sometimes cast myself as resident
Or fancy my identity as altered
Or, best of all, forget myself entirely,
Becoming yet another paper vessel
Floating in a common, human stream.
From that delectable hallucination,
Which bears the lure and danger of a dream,
I'm soon enough awakened: *You're the Yank
From Idaho. Whatd'ya hear from home?
Ya know, I have a cousin in Chicago. . .*
By all such enquiries and salutations,
Heard recurrently in Connor's pub

Amidst the pipe-smoke and the smell of Guinness,
Am I protected from my own delusions,
Though in the end not wholly satisfied.
Conceived by staunch Midwestern Methodists
And reared a Christian in a river town,
Companioned as a child by fields of corn
And menaced by a temperamental river,
Am I forever to be understood
As but the minted product of those forces,
Its features formal and indelible,
Its image fixed, as on a wooden nickel?
That I should venture to define myself
Against the waters of Liscannor Bay
Or see the image of my aspirations
In congeries of megalithic stone
Is no less plausible, it seems to me,
Than seeing in a Methodist retreat—
A basement dinner, long on casseroles
But short on zest and sensuality—
A fitting emblem of my inmost nature.
In truth, the listing ship on which I've sailed
For fifty years has kept itself afloat
By twists and turns too numerous to mention.
And of the several flags I've travelled under
The one most suited to my heart's unrest,
As to my temperament, is neither blue nor red
Nor green nor orange but a neutral white.
At home, if I can call it that, the wide
Waters of the river pass the bench
From which I watched the towboats pushing barges,
Aware, as best I could be, that the passing
Of coal and steel was not unlike the stream
Which would in time transport my aging frame
From Eastern Iowa to County Clare,
The waters here more turbulent by half
But not invaded by commercial vessels
Nor shadowed by a Methodist's compunctions.

II

No silence ever came more suddenly
Than what I happened on in mid-July,
Having bestirred myself to take a walk
Across the most intransigent of landscapes,
A coastal stretch comprised of creviced rock.
A boulder-meadow, someone might have called it,
Were not its contours quite the opposite
Of anything hospitable or kind
To lost sheep or ramblers like myself.
Conjure, if you will, a sandless desert
In tones of gray, its western edge converging
With bands of shifting, pewter cumuli,
Its eastern border reaching out to sea.
Within the cavities between the rocks
The colonies of violet lobelia
Sent up their quiet message of survival,
As if to contradict a larger voice
Which spoke of poverty and stark extinction.
What am I doing here? I asked myself,
Feeling the bumps of stone beneath my feet
And picturing myself, if only briefly,
As a Methodist's impression of a pilgrim,
A thick-heeled parody of penitence
In search of something not unlike atonement.
I might have made a tale of that vignette,
A fantasy replete with pieties,
My infant spirit nursed on paps of stone
And succoured by the silence of the place—
A silence even I, a connoisseur
Of quietude and dank monastic places,
Had never quite experienced before.
As it happened, that unbroken silence,
So rich in resonance if poor in speech,

So redolent of absence and abstention,
Was soon to be dismantled by the advent
Of startling company. At first a scarfed
Silhouette, a set of toiling shoulders.
Moving across a monochrome of stone,
Her presence soon took on its full proportions.
"A cold day," she said, as if the shawl
Wrapped securely round her coiled arms
Weren't evidence enough. Across its folds
Her black hair fell in runnels, flecked with gray.
"It is indeed," I said, and from that small
Aperture there flowed the usual
Banalities and customary phrases,
A stream of speech that widened as we walked,
Bearing in its waters bits of old
Biographies, the sticks if not the stones,
The stories that accompany a self
Over the boundaries of state and nation
And stay afloat through winding ways and decades.
From her I heard the story of a husband
Returned from war, his mind an aching muscle,
His heart a ghost. "A canister for drink,"
His well-wrought body swelled into a carcass
With which she lived, bruised but not disloyal,
But which at last she left, finding the stony
Soil of County Clare, where she was born,
A refuge from the dirty streets of Boston.
From me she heard the story of a wife
Gone off the rails—a noisy locomotive
Careening down a pebble-strewn embankment
And taking as its train the rumbling freight
Which her uncommon lust for acquisition
Had packed and lengthened, year by struggling year,
Its clanking boxcars bordered at the front
By her, and at the trailing end, by me.
"You were the red caboose?" my present consort

Made bold to ask. "I was indeed," I said,
"Though at the start I'd thought I was the tender."
Out of such assertions and exchanges,
Coloured, to be sure, by overtones
Of self-conceit and self-exoneration,
We fashioned something wider than ourselves
And less distinct—a fluid atmosphere
Within whose ambience those well-defined
Conglomerations called identities
Mingled in a shapeless, shifting wash
Which neither she nor I could call our own.
Over the course of many stony miles,
Accompanied by gulls and crashing surf,
We clambered over knee-high fieldstone walls
And helped each other over crevices,
Talking all the while. But only hours
Later, when the temperature was falling,
Did we compare our first, erroneous
Impressions. "You know," said she, "when I first heard
Your voice, I could have sworn that you were Irish."
And that, she added, was the honest truth,
Or as they say, "the holy alls of it."
I, in turn, confessed that in her speech
I'd heard the tones of an American,
Retuned, or so I'd thought, by County Clare
And tempered by the wear of Irish weather.
Was it the joint force of those disclosures
That parted us—or merely the signs of rain?
I couldn't say. But in their aftermath,
We went our ways, promising to meet
Again on some fortuitous occasion,
As though by meeting we had made the sign
Of infinity or cut a figure-eight
On water no more stable than ourselves,
On ice no less resurgent than our lives.

III

There you go, the waitresses declare,
Setting before us various concoctions,
As though a pair of eggs above a strip
Of bacon were an emblem of the one
Who ordered them, and souls could be divined
In what they eat. Wherever I have gone
Or may be going, I am not at all
Persuaded that a steaming bowl of porridge
Topped with walnuts and a spot of milk
Can signify my nature and direction
In their entirety. Better to read
The soggy hieroglyphics in my teacup
Or find in blots of ink a character
Which has for fifty years eluded me
And sometimes seems, in these unstable days
When nation-states are fashioning themselves
Out of the ruins of their former lives,
To be no more essential or substantial
Than nations given substance by a name
And peoples given credence by a label,
Albeit one recovered from the middens
And dusted off, almost as good as new.
Midwestern Protestant. American.
An *Iowan*. And, if you should insist,
A *Methodist*. Within such cumbersome
Containers, rarely thought of any more
But nonetheless sufficing to protect
A creature from the namelessness of chaos,
I have for decades lived and had my being.
But what, if anything, can *Iowa*
Mean to a cottager in County Clare?
And what can *Iowan* or *Methodist*
Mean to an aging sceptic like myself,

Who's read his share of social history
And can, for all his thrifty disposition
And curatorial temperament, imagine
A time when Iowans and Methodists
Were not? On lucid days, informed by light
Carousing in the lanes of the Atlantic,
I've seen those fleeting monikers as nothing
More or less than waves, recurrently
Arising and dissolving, taking with them
Whatever meanings they were trained to carry
And having, as it happens, no more claim
To permanence or glory than those placards
Hoisted at political conventions,
Declaiming to an audience of converts
The names *Virginia, Idaho, Ohio*.
Better, I think, to let that cardboard meet
Its destined end in furnace, dump, or landfill.
And better to regard my human form
As neither Iowan nor Protestant
But as the animal it really is,
A being forked and void of entourage,
If not yet mad or naked. Better, when all
Is said, to trace my origins to water—
Or, to be exact, the Mississippi,
That cold companion of my childhood,
Which Iowans of another time and colour
Called the waters' father. Even now,
A half a life removed from that abode
Of gar and carp, paddlefish and sturgeon,
I fashion out of mud and river water
My early history: myself as walker,
Not among the stones of County Clare
Nor on the moonstruck, sandless Flaggy Shore,
But on a sandbar littered with the dreck
Of human lust and human fecklessness.
There, amidst the bottlecaps and bottles,

The skeletons and cans, I found those agates—
Those scattered agates, dark as crusted blood—
Which would in time recall me to myself,
Having become a ring, a pair of cufflinks,
A tieclip where the currents of the river
Are mimed in amber, undulant striations.
I must have been eleven at the time.
How could I have guessed what would unfold
In forty years—or seen in those raw stones
An emblem of my own elusive nature,
Which I, for good or ill, would carry with me,
If only at the bottom of a box,
Concealed by ticket-stubs and photographs,
A broken watch, old coins, some slips of paper?
Whatever is unchanging in my nature
Could find its own reflection in those stones,
Those wine-dark ovals set in tarnished silver
And seeming to the world the least essential
And least defining item in my wardrobe—
Seeming, I should say, mere ornaments
Or what the world, in its unflagging zeal
For self-deceit, has deemed *accessories*.
I see them otherwise, as well I might.
And though it's only stones I'm looking into
I could be speaking to my own two eyes.

IV

I've always been the earliest of risers,
Though not, if truth be known, the most adept
At wakefulness—if what is meant by that
Is something not so different from a tomcat
Prowling in those alleys where the worst
Of memories are stashed in dented cans
And present spectres peer around the corners.
Ever alert for scents and signs of trouble,

That creature keeps his own nocturnal counsel
But in the daylight hours rests his case
And warms his ample torso on the hearthstone,
Ready to run or lunge, though feigning sleep.
My own mind is sometimes such a prowler
But is, more often, given to retreat
And in its strange proclivity for holes
And crumbling tunnels, often plays the groundhog,
Surfacing to forage, stand, and chew,
But more at home in lightless earthy cloisters.
Such was my demesne one Sunday morning,
When I awoke, aware of someone calling
And knocking at my door. In truth, I wanted
Nothing more than to be left alone
But found myself accosted by the one
Whom I had first encountered in the Burren,
Her hair a little frazzled from the wind,
Her lips chapped. Polite, though sleepy, I
Invited her to share a pot of tea
And by that gesture, wise or not so wise,
Admitted to the sanctum of my home
And my awareness something alien
But known, apart but not apart. Her call
Was social, she explained. But as she settled
Into a long unhappy monologue,
Her clenched hands a pedestal for her chin,
Her eyes on some invisible horizon,
It seemed as if she'd travelled from a place
Remote from mine—a place she'd carried with her
And laid, in jagged pieces, on my table.
She talked of convent schools and brutal nuns,
Of censored books and priests without vocation,
A pious lecher on a pilgrim train,
A schoolboy caned for venturing the word
Body in an essay. Such was the state
And the unbending temper of the country
To which she had returned, for good or ill,

And which she loved, for all its plaster statues,
Its narrow creeds and broad hypocrisies.
Replenishing her tea and listening
To attitudes and judgments not my own,
I felt as if the sleep from which I'd wakened
Had been invaded by a foreign power
And all that I was not had come to greet me.
Her brow contracted and her eyes took on
The look of someone waiting for an answer.
With what unseemly stories might I counter
Her visions of a national distemper?
Giving it my best, I conjured up
American *exempla*: a country club
Whose by-laws, vague but efficacious, placed
The darker races well beyond the Pale
Of sporting fellowship; a flaming cross
Ignited on a sympathiser's lawn
In Iowa, where such things never happen;
The story of a minister who proffered
Unwelcome truths to Christian gentlemen
And reaped as his reward a broken rib,
A battered ear and multiple abrasions.
"Bigotry is bigotry," I said,
Whether it happen here or over there.
But in the amber light of early morning
Streaming across my splintered kitchen table,
It seemed that as I summoned up those stories
Out of a chamber better left unlit,
I was uncovering a boundary
And sketching in the early morning air
A native self, a national enclosure.
I am of Ireland, she might have said,
For all her heated, crackling disapproval,
Her flattened brogue, her dozen years in Boston.
And I, I might have truthfully replied,
For all my travels and my trafficking
In Irish ways, *am of America*.

V

  Hear it as undulant courante,
Whose formal pattern changes by the second,
Revealing to the world and to oneself
The vagaries and checks, the graceful turns
And not-so-graceful lurchings of the spirit,
Which, had it never ventured such a caper,
Had never known itself. To that bold dance,
Which once was called the making of a soul
And now is called the finding of a self,
I pay the homage of an ardent mind.
Am I no more than that imagined man
Whom I've invented, not to spare myself
The old constraints of county, state, and country
But merely to be free of those compulsions
Which come with being what you've always been
Or think you've been—a being twice defined
By place and parentage, its image stamped
And dated? *There you go*, that coin declares
To all who have an interest in the matter.
But am I not entitled to envision
A being neither struck nor carved on stone
By accidents of lineage, place, and nation?
Hear it as the pulse of generation,
That stirring at the centre of the heart,
Where sometimes in the evenings I repair,
As eager for the heart's arcane reportage
As for the suet of the evening news.
Warming my damp feet before the fire,
I sometimes suffer glimpses of a self
Beholden not to eastern Iowa
Nor to the foreign stones of County Clare
Nor even to its own unbounded nature
But wandering from spring to plain to delta,
Itself a wave in swift, unending water.

And sometimes in my reveries I'm joined
By my astute companion from the Burren,
Whose name, if I may speak it now, is Maire.
Hearing, as I often do, her stories
Of Irish hardships, dreams, and peccadilloes,
I sometimes travel freely to those places
Of which she speaks, becoming now a farmer
And now a priest, and now an Irish lover.
From time to time, our conversation turns
To that impenetrable conundrum
Of who we are, or were, or might become
Were circumstance consistent with desire.
And when she asks me, as she sometimes does,
To tell her in a nutshell what I *want*,
Or what, if I could have it, I would *have*,
I find myself adopting in my speech,
As in my turn of thought, her own inflections.
The holy alls of it, I want to say,
Referring to a self I've yet to see
But have, on certain nights, intuited—
A self without the usual partitions
Dividing it from leaf and lake and stone,
As from its neighbouring inhabitants
And any colour other than its own.
To think of such a self, as thin as silk
And no less porous, is to entertain
A solemn mystery, though not the kind
Accompanied by thurible or cantor
Or pondered mightily from lofty pulpits.
I see it rather as a stormy day
Without the storm, the treetops undulant,
The hillsides ready for a blast of rain.
And when I think of it, it's not a sacred
Text that comes to mind, nor yet a vision
Of angels loitering around an altar
But something altogether natural—

A sky where clouds are forming and unforming
Even as they pass. And add to that
The kestrel's flight, its attitude as clear
And purposeful as any sculpted form,
Its veerings no less strange for being familiar,
Its cry no less remote for being known.

NOTES

"Lincoln's Hands": Leonard Wells Volk's *Life Mask and Hands of Abraham Lincoln* (1860) is housed in the Memorial Art Gallery in Rochester, New York. The sentence from Lincoln's letters appears in his letter to General Ulysses S. Grant, July 13, 1863. See *Selected Writings and Speeches of Abraham Lincoln*, ed. T. Harry Williams (Hendricks House, 1980).

"The Swinging Door": In *Zen Mind, Beginner's Mind*, Shunryu Suzuki likens the self to a swinging door: "What we call 'I' is just a swinging door which moves when we inhale and when we exhale. It just moves; that is all. When your mind is pure and calm enough to follow this movement, there is nothing: no 'I,' no world, no mind nor body; just a swinging door."

"Remembering Peace": Thich Nhat Hanh, the Vietnamese Zen master, poet, and peace activist, conducted a meditative retreat at the Omega Institute in Rhinebeck, New York in October, 1995.

"Westward": this poem alludes to Hayden Carruth's collection *Tell Me Again How the White Heron Rises and Flies Across the Nacreous River at Twilight Toward the Distant Islands* (New Directions, 1989).

"The Holy Alls": This poem may best be read as an epilogue to my book-length poem *Midcentury* (Salmon 1997). The speaker is an American lexicographer living in the West of Ireland in the 1950s.